G000057098

To

_____

From

_____

Date

_____

Choose Joy!

inspiration for your heart

Ellie Claire
gift & paper expressions

Ellie Claire® Gift & Paper Expressions
Franklin, TN 37067
EllieClaire.com
Ellie Claire is a registered trademark of Worthy Media, Inc.

Choose Joy!
© 2018 by Ellie Claire
Published by Ellie Claire, an imprint of Worthy Publishing Group,
a division of Worthy Media, Inc.

ISBN 978-1-63326-202-7

Stock or custom editions of Ellie Claire titles may be purchased in bulk for educational,
business, ministry, fundraising, or sales promotional use. For information, please e-mail
info@EllieClaire.com

Cover and interior design by Jeff Jansen | AestheticSoup.net

Printed in China

1 2 3 4 5 6 7 8 9 –HaHa–23 22 21 20 19 18

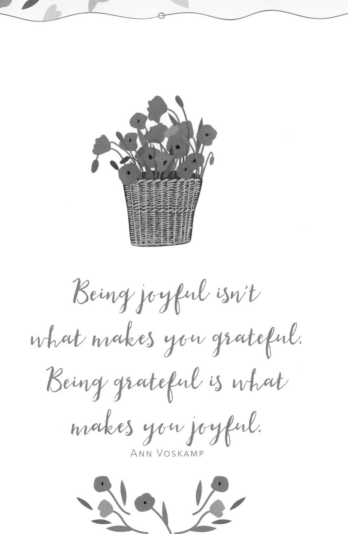

Being joyful isn't
what makes you grateful.
Being grateful is what
makes you joyful.

ANN VOSKAMP

Eternal Hope

Hope floods my heart with delight!
Running on air, mad with life, dizzy, reeling,
upward I mount—faith is sight, life is feeling....
I am immortal! I know it! I feel it!

MARGARET WITTER FULLER

Life is what we are alive to.
It is not length but breadth....
Be alive to...goodness, kindness, purity,
love, history, poetry, music, flowers,
stars, God, and eternal hope.

MALTBIE D. BABCOCK

He who breathes into our hearts
the heavenly hope will not deceive or fail us
when we press forward to its realization.

L. B. COWMAN

Hope sees the invisible, feels the intangible, and achieves
the impossible. When all my plans and hopes are fading like
a shadow, when all my dreams lie crumbled at my feet, I will
look up and know the night will bring tomorrow, and that
my Lord will bring me what I need.

GLORIA GAITHER

*I pray also that the eyes of your heart
may be enlightened in order that you may
know the hope to which he has called you.*

EPHESIANS 1:18 NIV

Source of Wonder

Dear Lord, grant me the grace of wonder.
Surprise me, amaze me, awe me in every crevice
of Your universe.... Each day enrapture me
with Your marvelous things without number.
I do not ask to see the reason for it all;
I ask only to share the wonder of it all.

JOSHUA ABRAHAM HESCHEL

May our lives be illumined
by the steady radiance renewed daily,
of a wonder, the source of which
is beyond reason.

DAG HAMMARSKJÖLD

I would maintain that thanks are
the highest form of thought,
and that gratitude is happiness
doubled by wonder.

G. K. CHESTERTON

The love of the Father is like a sudden rain shower
that will pour forth when you least expect it,
catching you up into wonder and praise.

RICHARD J. FOSTER

*I will give thanks to the LORD
with all my heart;
I will tell of all Your wonders.
I will be glad and exult in You;
I will sing praise to Your name,
O Most High.*

PSALM 9:1–2 NASB

Child of God

To the children of God there stands,
behind all that changes and can change,
only one unchangeable joy. That is God.

HANNAH WHITALL SMITH

He only is the Maker of all things near and far;
He paints the wayside flower,
He lights the evening star;
the wind and waves obey Him,
by Him the birds are fed; much more to us,
His children, He gives our daily bread.

MATTHIAS CLAUDIUS

When we call on God, He bends down His ear to listen,
as a father bends down to listen to his little child.

ELIZABETH CHARLES

Remember, as His precious child,
you are very special to God. He has promised
to complete the good work He has begun in you.
As you continue to grow in Him,
He will make you a blessing to others.

See how very much our Father loves us,
for he calls us his children,
and that is what we are!

1 JOHN 3:1 NLT

Faithful Guide

Slippings and strayings there will be,
no doubt, but the everlasting arms are beneath us;
we shall be caught, rescued, restored.
This is God's promise; this is how good He is.
And our self-distrust, while keeping us humble,
must not cloud the joy with which
we lean on our faithful covenant God.

J. I. PACKER

God, who has led you safely on so far,
will lead you on to the end.
Be altogether at rest in the loving
holy confidence which you ought to have
in His heavenly Providence.

FRANCIS DE SALES

Joy comes from knowing God loves me
and knows who I am and where I'm going...
that my future is secure as I rest in Him.

JAMES DOBSON

Because of the tender mercy
of our God, with which
the Sunrise from on high
will visit us, to shine upon those
who sit in darkness...to guide
our feet into the way of peace.

LUKE 1:78–79 NASB

Love One Another

There is the whisper of His love,
the joy of His presence, and the shining of His face,
for those who love Jesus for Himself alone.

SUSAN B. STRACHAN

You who have received so much love
share it with others. Love others the way
that God has loved you, with tenderness.

MOTHER TERESA

Every single act of love bears the imprint of God.

Love means to love that which is unlovable,
or it is no virtue at all; forgiving means to pardon
that which is unpardonable, or it is no virtue at all—
and to hope means hoping when things
are hopeless, or it is no virtue at all.

G. K. CHESTERTON

We must strengthen, defend, preserve, and comfort
each other. We must love one another.

JOHN WINTHROP

Dear friends, since God so loved us,
we also ought to love one another....
If we love one another, God lives in us
and his love is made complete in us.

1 JOHN 4:11–12 NIV

Every Need

Jesus Christ has brought every need, every joy,
every gratitude, every hope of ours before God.
He accompanies us and brings us into the presence of God.

DIETRICH BONHOEFFER

God wants nothing from us except our needs,
and these furnish Him with room to display His bounty
when He supplies them freely.... Not what I have,
but what I do not have, is the first point of contact
between my soul and God.

CHARLES H. SPURGEON

When life becomes difficult, when cracks spread
through our existence and our strength
seems to leak out, fill the gaps with hope.
Like gold adorning distressed ancient art,
hope will reinforce, add value, and reveal more beauty.

BARBARA FARMER

The "air" which our souls need also envelops all of us
at all times and on all sides. God is round about us...
on every hand, with many-sided and all-sufficient grace.

OLE HALLESBY

As for me, I will sing about your strength;
I will praise your loyal love in the morning.
For you are my refuge and my place
of shelter when I face trouble.

PSALM 59:16 NET

Joy is the
serious business
of heaven.

C. S. LEWIS

Miracle of Grace

Grace creates liberated laughter. The grace of God...is beautiful, and it radiates joy and awakens humor.

KARL BARTH

Oh, make us more aware, dear God,
Of little daily graces
That come to us with sweet surprise
From never-dreamed-of places.

HELEN STEINER RICE

In the presence of hope, faith is born. In the presence
of faith, love becomes a possibility!
In the presence of love, miracles happen!

ROBERT SCHULLER

The beauty of grace...is that it meets us where we are
and gives us what we don't deserve.

CHARLES R. SWINDOLL

Where there is faith, there is love.
Where there is love, there is peace.
Where there is peace, there is God.
Where there is God, there is no need.

God is able to make all grace abound to you,
so that always having all sufficiency
in everything, you may have an abundance
for every good deed.

2 CORINTHIANS 9:8 NASB

By Love Alone

By love alone is God enjoyed;
by love alone delighted in, by love alone approached
and admired. His nature requires love.

THOMAS TRAHERNE

There is an essential connection between experiencing God,
loving God, and trusting God. You will trust God only
as much as you love Him, and you will love Him to the extent
you have touched Him, rather that He has touched you.

BRENNAN MANNING

We have a Father in heaven...who loves His children
as He loves His only-begotten Son, and whose very joy
and delight it is to...help them at all times
and under all circumstances.

GEORGE MUELLER

Love does not allow lovers to belong anymore
to themselves, but they belong only to the Beloved.

DIONYSIUS

Love the LORD your God with all your heart,
all your soul, and all your strength.

DEUTERONOMY 6:5 NLT

A Life of Prayer

They who seek the throne of grace find that throne in every place; if we live a life of prayer, God is present everywhere.

OLIVER HOLDEN

Be joyful in hope, patient in affliction, faithful in prayer.

ROMANS 12:12 NIV

Part of our job is to expect that, if we are attentive and willing, God will "give us prayer," will give us the things we need, "our daily bread," to heal and grow in love.

ROBERTA BONDI

If the Lord be with us, we have no cause to fear. His eye is upon us, His arm over us, His ear open to our prayer—His grace sufficient, His promise unchangeable.

JOHN NEWTON

Our Father in heaven, we honor your holy name. We ask that your kingdom will come now. May your will be done here on earth, just as it is in heaven. Give us our food again today, as usual, and forgive us our sins, just as we have forgiven those who have sinned against us. Don't bring us into temptation, but deliver us from the Evil One. Amen.

MATTHEW 6:9–13 TLB

Unique Gifts

God has a wonderful plan for each person He has chosen.
He knew even before He created this world what beauty He
would bring forth from our lives.

LOUISE B. WYLY

This is the real gift: you have been given the breath of life,
designed with a unique, one-of-a-kind soul that exists
forever—the way that you choose to live it doesn't change
the fact that you've been given the gift of "being," now
and forever. Priceless in value, you are handcrafted by God.
He has a personal design and plan for each of us.

WENDY MOORE

Everyone has a unique role to fill in the world
and is important in some respect. Everyone,
including and perhaps especially you, is indispensable.

NATHANIEL HAWTHORNE

God gives us all gifts, special abilities
that we are entrusted with developing
in order to help serve Him and serve others.

God has given each of you a gift from his
great variety of spiritual gifts. Use them
well to serve one another.

1 PETER 4:10 NLT

Enfolded in Peace

I will let God's peace infuse every part of today.
As the chaos swirls and life's demands pull at me
on all sides, I will breathe in God's peace
that surpasses all understanding. He has promised
that He would set within me a peace too deeply planted
to be affected by unexpected or exhausting demands.

Calm me, O Lord, as you stilled the storm,
Still me, O Lord, keep me from harm.
Let all the tumult within me cease,
Enfold me, Lord, in your peace.

CELTIC TRADITIONAL

God cannot give us a happiness and peace apart from Himself, because it is not there. There is no such thing.

C. S. LEWIS

God came to us because God wanted to join us on the road, to listen to our story, and to help us realize that we are not walking in circles but moving toward the house of peace and joy.

HENRI J. M. NOUWEN

Do not be anxious about anything. Instead, in every situation, through prayer and petition with thanksgiving, tell your requests to God. And the peace of God that surpasses all understanding will guard your hearts and minds in Christ Jesus.

PHILIPPIANS 4:6-7 NET

The Sacred Ordinary

Much of what is sacred is hidden in the ordinary,
everyday moments of our lives. To see something
of the sacred in those moments takes slowing down
so we can live our lives more reflectively.

KEN GIRE

Lord...remind me daily that choosing to be happy
is an option. May I find my strength in Your joy.

KIM BOYCE

If we have never been amazed by the very fact that we exist,
we are squandering the greatest fact of all.

WILL DURANT

We encounter God in the ordinariness of life,
not in the search for spiritual highs and extraordinary,
mystical experiences, but in our simple presence in life.

BRENNAN MANNING

Simplicity will enable you to leap lightly.
Increasingly you will find yourself living in a state of grace,
finding...the sacred in the ordinary,
the mystical in the mundane.

DAVID YOUNT

*You will make known to me
the path of life; in Your presence
is fullness of joy; in Your right hand
there are pleasures forever.*

PSALM 16:11 NASB

The fruit of the Spirit is...joy.

GALATIANS 5:22

Settled in Solitude

The wonder of living is held within the beauty of silence,
the glory of sunlight...the sweetness
of fresh spring air, the quiet strength of earth,
and the love that lies at the very root of all things.

Settle yourself in solitude and you will come upon Him.

TERESA OF AVILA

Peace with God brings the peace of God.
It is a peace that settles our nerves, fills our mind,
floods our spirit, and in the midst of the uproar around us,
gives us the assurance that everything is all right.

BOB MUMFORD

We must drink deeply from the very Source
the deep calm and peace of interior quietude
and refreshment of God, allowing the pure water
of divine grace to flow plentifully
and unceasingly from the Source itself.

MOTHER TERESA

Whoever drinks of the water that I will give
him shall never thirst; but the water that I
will give him will become in him a well
of water springing up to eternal life.

JOHN 4:14 NASB

Dreams Fulfilled

Lift up your eyes. Your heavenly Father waits to bless you—
in inconceivable ways to make your life
what you never dreamed it could be.

ANNE ORTLUND

God is not an elusive dream or a phantom to chase,
but a divine person to know. He does not avoid us,
but seeks us. When we seek Him,
the contact is instantaneous.

NEVA COYLE

The human heart has hidden treasures, in secret kept,
in silence sealed;—the thoughts, the hopes, the dreams,
the pleasures, whose charms were broken if revealed.

CHARLOTTE BRONTË

God created us with an overwhelming desire to soar....
He designed us to be tremendously productive
and "to mount up with wings like eagles," realistically
dreaming of what He can do with our potential.

CAROL KENT

I will give you treasures hidden in the
darkness, secret riches; and you will know
that I am doing this — I, the Lord,
the God of Israel, the one who
calls you by your name.

ISAIAH 45:3 TLB

Someone Special

The Creator thinks enough of you to have sent
Someone very special so that you might have life—
abundantly, joyfully, completely, and victoriously.

When we love someone, we want to be with them,
and we view their love for us with great honor even
if they are not a person of great status. For this reason—
and not because of our great status—God values our love.
So much, in fact, that He suffered greatly on our behalf.

JOHN CHRYSOSTOM

What brings joy to the heart is not so much
the friend's gifts as the friend's love.

AELRED OF RIEVAULX

Someone speaks a word of hope to a discouraged soul,
and light shines in his prison.

RUTH ANN POLSTON

One of Jesus's specialties is to make somebodies
out of nobodies.

HENRIETTA MEARS

God demonstrates His own love toward us,
in that while we were yet sinners,
Christ died for us.

ROMANS 5:8 NASB

God Listens

Ah! How often…has God kissed you
at the beginning of prayer,
and spoken peace to you in the middle of prayer,
and filled you with joy and assurance
upon the close of prayer!

THOMAS BROOKS

We know that God…listens to the godly person
who does his will.

JOHN 9:31 NIV

We come this morning—like empty pitchers
to a full fountain, with no merits of our own, O Lord—
open up a window of heaven… And listen this morning.

JAMES WELDON JOHNSON

God listens in compassion and love, just like we do when our children come to us. He delights in our presence.

Richard J. Foster

Be still, and in the quiet moments, listen to the voice of your heavenly Father. His words can renew your spirit...no one knows you and your needs like He does.

Janet L. Weaver Smith

I love the LORD because he hears my voice
and my prayer for mercy.
Because he bends down to listen,
I will pray as long as I have breath!

Psalm 116:1–2 NLT

Grace Revealed

Look deep within yourself and recognize what brings life
and grace into your heart. It is this that can be shared
with those around you. You are loved by God.
This is an inspiration to love.

CHRISTOPHER DE VINCK

All God's glory and beauty come from within,
and there He delights to dwell. His visits there are frequent,
His conversation sweet, His comforts refreshing,
His peace passing all understanding.

THOMAS À KEMPIS

The Lord gives you the experience of enjoying His presence.
He touches you, and His touch is so delightful that,
more than ever, you are drawn inwardly to Him.

JEANNE GUYON

You are a...people for God's own possession,
so that you may proclaim the excellencies
[the wonderful deeds and virtues
and perfections] of Him who called you
out of darkness into His marvelous light.

1 PETER 2:9 AMP

Countless Beauties

The beauty of the earth, the beauty of the sky, the order of
the stars, the sun, the moon...their very loveliness is their
confession of God: for who made these lovely mutable
things, but He who is Himself unchangeable beauty?

AUGUSTINE

May God give you eyes to see beauty
only the heart can understand.

All the world is an utterance of the Almighty.
Its countless beauties, its exquisite adaptations,
all speak to you of Him.

PHILLIPS BROOKS

All the beautiful sentiments in the world
weigh less than a simple lovely action.

JAMES RUSSELL LOWELL

From the world we see, hear, and touch,
we behold inspired visions that reveal God's glory.
In the sun's light, we catch warm rays of grace and glimpse
His eternal design. In the birds' song, we hear His voice
and it reawakens our desire for Him. At the wind's touch,
we feel His Spirit and sense our eternal existence.

Oh, worship the LORD
in the beauty of holiness!

PSALM 96:9 NKJV

Savor little glimpses of God's goodness and His majesty, thankful for the gift of them. The secret to joy is to keep seeking God where we doubt He is.

ANN VOSKAMP

Ever Present

When I walk by the wayside, He is along with me....
Amid all my forgetfulness of Him, He never forgets me.

THOMAS CHALMERS

There's not a tint that paints the rose or decks the lily fair,
or marks the humblest flower that grows,
but God has placed it there.... There's not a place
on earth's vast round, in ocean's deep or air,
where love and beauty are not found,
for God is everywhere.

At every moment, God is calling your name
and waiting to be found. To each cry of "Oh Lord,"
God answers, "I am here."

They who seek the throne of grace
Find that throne in every place;
If we live a life of prayer,
God is present everywhere.

OLIVER HOLDEN

God is our refuge and strength,
an ever-present help in trouble.
Therefore we will not fear.

PSALM 46:1–2 NIV

Hold Fast Your Dreams

Hold fast your dreams! Within your heart keep one still,
secret spot where dreams may go and, sheltered so,
may thrive and grow.... O keep a place apart,
within your heart, for little dreams to go!

LOUISE DRISCOLL

Life itself, every bit of health that we enjoy,
every hour of...free enjoyment, the ability
to see, to hear, to speak, to think, and to imagine—
all this comes from the hand of God.

BILLY GRAHAM

Allow your dreams a place in your prayers and plans.
God-given dreams can help you move
into the future He is preparing for you.

Always stay connected to people
and seek out things that bring you joy.
Dream with abandon. Pray confidently.

BARBARA JOHNSON

Hope is the ability to hear the music of the future....

Faith is having the courage to dance to it today.

PETER KUZMIC

A dream fulfilled is a tree of life.

PROVERBS 13:12 NLT

Simple Wonders

A fiery sunset, tiny pansies by the wayside,
the sound of raindrops tapping on the roof—
what an extraordinary delight to notice
simple wonders! With wide eyes and full hearts,
we have the opportunity to cherish
what others have missed and to thank God for them.

The wonder of our Lord is that He is so accessible to us in
the common things of our lives: the cup of water...
breaking of the bread...welcoming children into our arms...
fellowship over a meal...giving thanks. A simple attitude
of caring, listening, and lovingly telling the truth.

NANCIE CARMICHAEL

If God is here for us and not elsewhere,
then in fact *this place* is holy
and *this moment* is sacred.

ISABEL ANDERS

God still draws near to us in the ordinary,
commonplace, everyday experiences and places....
He comes in surprising ways.

HENRY GARIEPY

*O give thanks to the LORD, for He is good;
for His lovingkindness endures forever.*

PSALM 118:29 AMP

Eternal Moments

Friendships, family ties, the companionship
of little children, an autumn forest flung in prodigality
against a deep blue sky, the intricate design
and haunting fragrance of a flower, the counterpoint
of a Bach fugue or the melodic line of a Beethoven sonata,
the fluted note of bird song, the glowing glory of a sunset:
the world is aflame with things of eternal moment.

E. MARGARET CLARKSON

Always new. Always exciting. Always full of promise.
The mornings of our lives, each a personal daily miracle!

GLORIA GAITHER

Sunset

The day is done,
the sun has set,
yet light still tints the sky;
my heart stands still
in reverence,
for God is passing by.

RUTH ALLA WAGER

Often it's in the middle of the most mundane task
that He lets us know He is there with us. We realize,
then, that there can be no "ordinary" moments
for people who live their lives with Jesus.

MICHAEL CARD

Where morning dawns and evening fades
you call forth songs of joy.

PSALM 65:8 NIV

Watchful Care

He paints the lily of the field, perfumes each lily bell;
if He so loves the little flowers, I know He loves me well.

MARIA STRAUS

The LORD is in his holy Temple; the LORD still rules
from heaven. He watches everything closely,
examining every person on earth.... For the righteous LORD
loves justice. The virtuous will see his face.

PSALM 11:4, 7 NLT

God's in His heaven—all's right with the world!

ROBERT BROWNING

God cares for the world He created, from the rising
of a nation to the falling of the sparrow.
Everything in the world lies under the watchful gaze
of His providential eyes, from the numbering of the days
of our life to the numbering of the hairs on our head.
When we look at the world from that perspective,
it produces within us a response of reverence.

KEN GIRE

*He will give His angels
charge concerning you,
to guard you in all your ways.*
PSALM 91:11 NASB

Destiny

Recognizing who we are in Christ and aligning
our life with God's purpose for us gives a sense of destiny....
It gives form and direction to our life.

JEAN FLEMING

When we live life centered around what others like,
feel, and say, we lose touch with our own identity.
I am an eternal being, created by God.
I am an individual with purpose. It's not what I get from life,
but who I am, that makes the difference.

NEVA COYLE

God has a purpose for your life
and no one else can take your place.

I believe that nothing that happens to me is meaningless,
and that it is good for us all that it should be so....
As I see it, I'm here for some purpose.

DIETRICH BONHOEFFER

When the world around us staggers from lack of direction,
God offers purpose, hope, and certainty.

GLORIA GAITHER

*May the favor of the Lord our God rest upon
us; establish the work of our hands for us.*

PSALM 90:17 NIV

It is always wise
to stop wishing for things
long enough to enjoy
the fragrance of those
now flowering.

PATRICE GIFFORD

Totally Aware

No one passes through any area of life,
happy or tragic, without the attention of God with him.

EUGENIA PRICE

You saw how the LORD your God cared for you
all along the way as you traveled through the wilderness,
just as a father cares for his child.

DEUTERONOMY 1:31 NLT

God reads the secrets of the heart.
God reads the most intimate feelings,
even those which we are not aware of.

JEAN-NICHOLAS GROU

Because God is responsible for our welfare,
we are told to cast all our care upon Him, for He cares for us.
God says, "I'll take the burden—don't give it a thought—
leave it to Me." God is keenly aware that we are
dependent upon Him for life's necessities.

BILLY GRAHAM

Casting all your cares [all your anxieties,
all your worries, and all your concerns,
once and for all] on Him, for He cares
about you [with deepest affection,
and watches over you very carefully].

1 PETER 5:7 AMP

Glorious Handiwork

He made you so you could share in His creation,
could love and laugh and know Him.

TED GRIFFEN

You are a creation of God unequaled anywhere
in the universe.... Thank Him for yourself
and then for all the rest of His glorious handiwork.

NORMAN VINCENT PEALE

God's love is like a river springing up in the Divine
Substance and flowing endlessly through His creation,
filling all things with life and goodness and strength.

THOMAS MERTON

The huge dome of the sky is...the most like infinity.
When God made space and worlds that move in space,
and clothed our world with air, and gave us such eyes
and such imaginations as those we have, He knew
what the sky would mean to us.... We cannot be certain
that this was not indeed one of the chief purposes
for which Nature was created.

C. S. LEWIS

*The heavens declare his righteousness,
and all the people see his glory.*

PSALM 97:6 KJV

In His Likeness

The God of the universe—the One who created everything
and holds it all in His hand—created each of us in His image,
to bear His likeness, His imprint. It is only when Christ dwells
within our hearts, radiating the pure light of His love
through our humanity, that we discover who we are
and what we were intended to be.

God's children who joyously know and claim
who they are and whose they are
will be most likely to manifest the family likeness,
just because they know they are His children.

ALICE CHAPIN

Made in His image, we can have real meaning,
and we can have real knowledge
through what He has communicated to us.

FRANCIS SCHAEFFER

In the very beginning it was God who formed us
by His Word. He made us in His own image.
God was spirit and He gave us a spirit so that He could
come into us and mingle His own life with our life.

JEANNE GUYON

You have everything when you have
Christ, and you are filled with God
through your union with Christ.

COLOSSIANS 2:10 TLB

Happiness and Gratitude

Our inner happiness depends not
on what we experience but on the degree
of our gratitude to God, whatever the experience.

ALBERT SCHWEITZER

So wait before the Lord. Wait in the stillness.
And in that stillness, assurance will come to you.
You will know that you are heard...you will hear
quiet words spoken to you yourself,
perhaps to your grateful surprise and refreshment.

AMY CARMICHAEL

It is not how much we have, but how much we enjoy,
that makes happiness.

CHARLES H. SPURGEON

Gratitude consists in a watchful, minute attention
to the particulars of our state, and to the multitude
of God's gifts, taken one by one. It fills us with
a consciousness that God loves and cares for us,
even to the least event and smallest need of life.

HENRY EDWARD MANNING

*I will bless the LORD
at all times: his praise shall
continually be in my mouth.*

PSALM 34:1 KJV

A Firsthand Experience

Listening to God is a firsthand experience....
God invites *you* to vacation in His splendor.
He invites *you* to feel the touch of His hand.
He invites *you* to feast at His table.
He wants to spend time with *you*.

Max Lucado

Prayer is everywhere.... Prayer is language
used to respond to the most that has been said to us,
with the potential for saying all that is in us.

Eugene Peterson

In both simple and eloquent ways, our infinite God personally reveals glimpses of Himself in the finite.

In extravagance of soul we seek His face.
In generosity of heart, we glean His gentle touch.
In excessiveness of spirit, we love Him
and His love comes back to us a hundredfold.

TRICIA McCARY RHODES

God is faithful, through whom you were called into fellowship with His Son, Jesus Christ our Lord.

1 CORINTHIANS 1:9 NASB

What Matters

The God who created, names, and numbers the stars
in the heavens also numbers the hairs of my head....
He pays attention to very big things and to very small ones.
What matters to me matters to Him,
and that changes my life.

ELISABETH ELLIOT

What really matters is what happens in us, not to us.

JAMES KENNEDY

One hundred years from today your present income
will be inconsequential. One hundred years from now
it won't matter if you got that big break....
It will greatly matter that you knew God.

DAVID SHIBLEY

What matters supremely is not the fact that I know God,
but the larger fact which underlies it—
the fact that He knows me. I am graven on the palms
of His hands. I am never out of His mind.
All my knowledge of Him depends
on His sustained initiative in knowing me.
I know Him because He first knew me,
and continues to know me.

J. I. PACKER

Do not fear, for I have redeemed you;
I have called you by name; you are Mine!

ISAIAH 43:1 NASB

Where the soul is full
of peace and joy,
outward surroundings
and circumstances
are of comparatively
little account.

HANNAH WHITALL SMITH

Shining Through

As a countenance is made beautiful
by the soul's shining through it,
so the world is beautiful by the shining through it of God.

FREDERICH HEINRICH JACOBI

Don't ever let yourself get so busy that you miss
those little but important extras in life—the beauty of a day,
the smile of a friend, the serenity of a quiet moment alone.
For it is often life's smallest pleasures and gentlest joys
that make the biggest and most lasting difference.
Someone said to me once that we can see
the features of God in a single smile.
Look for that smile in the people you meet.

CHRISTOPHER DE VINCK

Dear Lord...shine through me, and be so in me that every soul I come in contact with may feel Your presence in my soul.... Let me thus praise You in the way You love best, by shining on those around me.

JOHN HENRY NEWMAN

And the Lord—who is the Spirit—
makes us more and more like him
as we are changed into his glorious image.

2 CORINTHIANS 3:18 NLT

The Goodness of God

The goodness of God is infinitely more wonderful
than we will ever be able to comprehend.

A. W. TOZER

All that is good, all that is true, all that is beautiful,
all that is beneficent, be it great or small,
be it perfect or fragmentary, natural as well as supernatural,
moral as well as material, comes from God.

JOHN HENRY NEWMAN

We walk without fear, full of hope
and courage and strength to do His will,
waiting for the endless good which He is always giving
as fast as He can get us able to take it in.

GEORGE MACDONALD

Oh, put God to the test and see
how kind he is! See for yourself
the way his mercies shower down on all
who trust in him. If you belong to the Lord,
reverence him; for everyone
who does this has everything he needs.

PSALM 34:8–9 TLB

New Every Morning

Hold on, my child! Joy comes in the morning!
Weeping only lasts for the night....
The darkest hour means dawn is just in sight!

GLORIA GAITHER

O LORD, be gracious to us; we long for you.
Be our strength every morning,
our salvation in time of distress.

ISAIAH 33:2 NIV

Ah, Hope! what would life be, stripped of thy encouraging
smiles, that teach us to look behind the dark clouds
of today, for the golden beams that are to gild the morrow.

SUSANNA MOODIE

That is God's call to us—simply to be people who are content
to live close to Him and to renew the kind of life
in which the closeness is felt and experienced.

THOMAS MERTON

The faithful love of the LORD never ends!
His mercies never cease.
Great is his faithfulness;
his mercies begin afresh each morning.

LAMENTATIONS 3:22–23 NLT

His Beautiful World

The God who holds the whole world in His hands
wraps Himself in the splendor of the sun's light
and walks among the clouds.

Forbid that I should walk through Thy beautiful world
with unseeing eyes: Forbid that the lure of the market-place
should ever entirely steal my heart away from the love
of the open acres and the green trees: Forbid that under
the low roof of workshop or office or study
I should ever forget Thy great overarching sky.

JOHN BAILLIE

Our Creator would never have made such lovely days,
and given us the deep hearts to enjoy them,
above and beyond all thought,
unless we were meant to be immortal.

NATHANIEL HAWTHORNE

May your life become one of glad and unending praise
to the Lord as you journey through this world.

TERESA OF AVILA

The whole earth is full of his glory.

ISAIAH 6:3 KJV

Footpath to Peace

To be glad of life, because it gives you the chance to love
and to work and to play and to look up at the stars;
to be satisfied with your possessions, but not contented
with yourself until you have made the best of them...
to think seldom of your enemies, often of your friends,
and every day of Christ; and to spend as much time
as you can, with body and with spirit in God's out-of-doors—
these are little guideposts on the footpath to peace.

HENRY VAN DYKE

[Jesus] brings hope, forgiveness, heart cleansing peace,
and power. He is our deliverer and coming King.

LUCILLE M. LAW

Only God gives true peace—a quiet gift He sets within us just when we think we've exhausted our search for it.

God's peace is joy resting. His joy is peace dancing.

F. F. BRUCE

The LORD will give strength to His people; the LORD will bless His people with peace.

PSALM 29:11 NKJV

Overflowing Praise

All enjoyment spontaneously overflows into praise....
The world rings with praise...walkers praising
the countryside, players praising their favorite game....
I think we delight to praise what we enjoy because
the praise not merely expresses but completes
the enjoyment; it is the appointed consummation.

C. S. LEWIS

Angels bright, heavens high,
waters deep, give God the praise.

CHRISTOPHER COLLINS

God's pursuit of praise from us and our pursuit
of pleasure in Him are one and the same pursuit.

JOHN PIPER

Earth, with her thousand voices, praises God.

SAMUEL TAYLOR COLERIDGE

We are called to witness, always with our lives
and sometimes with our words,
to the great things God has done for us.

HENRI J. M. NOUWEN

[God] stands fast as your rock, steadfast as your safeguard,
sleepless as your watcher, valiant as your champion.

CHARLES H. SPURGEON

Sing to God!... Exalt the one who rides
on the clouds! For the LORD is his name!
Rejoice before him!

PSALM 68:4 NET

A joyful spirit is like
a sunny day;
it sheds a brightness
over everything;
it sweetens our circumstances
and soothes our souls.

Faith Adventure

There will always be the unknown.
There will always be the unprovable.
But faith confronts those frontiers with a thrilling leap.
Then life becomes vibrant with adventure!

ROBERT SCHULLER

Faith means you want God and want to want nothing else....
In faith there is movement and development.
Each day something is new.

BRENNAN MANNING

Be joyful in hope, patient in affliction, faithful in prayer.

ROMANS 12:12 NIV

Faith sees the invisible, believes the incredible,
and receives the impossible.

God wants us to approach life, full of expectancy
that God is going to be at work in every situation
as we grow in our faith in Him.

COLIN URQUHART

Faith is not a sense, not sight, not reason,
but a taking God at His Word.

FAITH EVANS

With God all things are possible.

MARK 10:27 KJV

Always There

We need never shout across the spaces to an absent God.
He is nearer than our own soul,
closer than our most secret thoughts.

A. W. Tozer

God is always present in the temple of your heart...
His home. And when you come in to meet Him there,
you find that it is the one place of deep satisfaction
and joy where every longing is met.

God is the sunshine that warms us, the rain that melts away
the frost and waters the young plants. The presence of God
is a climate of strong and bracing love, always there.

Joan Arnold

Always be in a state of expectancy,
and see that you leave room for God to come in as He likes.

OSWALD CHAMBERS

God's hand is always there;
once you grasp it you'll never want to let go.

*How lovely are Your dwelling places,
O LORD of hosts! My soul longed and even
yearned for the courts of the LORD;
my heart and my flesh sing for joy
to the living God.... For a day in Your courts
is better than a thousand outside.*

PSALM 84:1–2, 10 NASB

A Life Worthwhile

I wish you humor and a twinkle in the eye. I wish you glory
and the strength to bear its burdens. I wish you sunshine on
your path and storms to season your journey.
I wish you peace—in the world in which you live
and in the smallest corner of the heart where truth is kept.
I wish you faith—to help define your living and your life.
More I cannot wish you—except perhaps love—
to make all the rest worthwhile.

ROBERT A. WARD

What makes life worthwhile is having a big
enough objective, something which catches
our imagination and lays hold of our allegiance....
What higher, more exalted, and more
compelling goal can there be than to know God?

J. I. PACKER

God is with us in the midst of our daily,
routine lives. In the middle of cleaning the house
or driving somewhere in the pickup.

MICHAEL CARD

*I consider everything a loss compared
to the surpassing greatness of knowing
Christ Jesus my Lord.*

PHILIPPIANS 3:8 NIV

Nothing but Grace

There is nothing but God's grace. We walk upon it;
we breathe it; we live and die by it;
it makes the nails and axles of the universe.

ROBERT LOUIS STEVENSON

Grace is no stationary thing, it is ever becoming.
It is flowing straight out of God's heart.
Grace does nothing but re-form and convey God.
Grace makes the soul conformable to the will of God.
God, the ground of the soul, and grace go together.

JOHANNES ECKHART

The grace of God means something like: Here is your life. You might never have been, but you are because the party wouldn't have been complete without you.

FREDERICK BUECHNER

Grace and gratitude belong together like heaven and earth. Grace evokes gratitude like the voice an echo. Gratitude follows grace as thunder follows lightning.

KARL BARTH

The LORD is compassionate and merciful, slow to get angry and filled with unfailing love.... He has removed our sins as far from us as the east is from the west.

PSALM 103:8, 12 NLT

An Inner Place

Slow down and enjoy life. It's not only the scenery
you miss by going too fast—you also miss the sense
of where you are going and why.

EDDIE CANTOR

Retire from the world each day to some private spot....
Stay in the secret place till the surrounding noises
begin to fade out of your heart
and a sense of God's presence envelops you.

A. W. TOZER

Within each of us there is an inner place where the living
God Himself longs to dwell, our sacred center of belief.

I will remember that when I give Him my heart,
God chooses to live within me—body and soul.
And I know He really is as close as breathing,
His very Spirit inside of me.

Love comes while we rest against our Father's chest.
Joy comes when we catch the rhythms of His heart.
Peace comes when we live in harmony with those rhythms.

KEN GIRE

I pray that out of his glorious riches he may strengthen you with power through his Spirit in your inner being.

EPHESIANS 3:16 NIV

In God's Thoughts

Tonight I will sleep beneath Your feet,
O Lord of the mountains and valleys, ruler of the trees
and vines. I will rest in Your love, with You protecting me
as a father protects his children, with You watching
over me as a mother watches over her children.
Then tomorrow the sun will rise and I will not know where I
am; but I know that You will guide my footsteps.

EARLY AMERICAN PRAYER

We have been in God's thought from all eternity,
and in His creative love, His attention never leaves us.

MICHAEL QUOIST

Life in the presence of God
should be known to us in conscious experience.
It is a life to be enjoyed every moment of every day.

A. W. TOZER

Many, O LORD my God, are the wonders
which You have done, and Your thoughts
toward us; there is none to compare with
You If I would declare and speak of them,
they would be too numerous to count.

PSALM 40:5 NASB

This is the day
which the LORD hath made;
we will rejoice
and be glad in it.

PSALM 118:24 KJV

Made for Joy

Our hearts were made for joy. Our hearts were made
to enjoy the One who created them. Too deeply planted
to be much affected by the ups and downs of life,
this joy is a knowing and a being known by our Creator.
He sets our hearts alight with radiant joy.

WENDY MOORE

If one is joyful, it means that one is faithfully living for God,
and that nothing else counts;
and if one gives joy to others one is doing God's work.
With joy without and joy within, all is well.

JANET ERSKINE STUART

Live for today but hold your hands open to tomorrow.
Anticipate the future and its changes with joy.
There is a seed of God's love in every event,
every circumstance, every unpleasant situation
in which you may find yourself.

BARBARA JOHNSON

The joy of the LORD is your strength.

NEHEMIAH 8:10 KJV

Contentment

If we are cheerful and contented, all nature smiles...
the flowers are more fragrant, the birds sing more sweetly,
and the sun, moon, and stars all appear more beautiful,
and seem to rejoice with us.

ORISON SWETT MARDEN

Godliness with contentment is great gain.
For we brought nothing into the world,
and we can take nothing out of it.
But if we have food and clothing,
we will be content with that.

1 TIMOTHY 6:6–8 NIV

Contentment is not the fulfillment of what you want,
but the realization of how much you already have.

The miracle of joy is this: It happens when
there is no apparent reason for it.
Circumstances may call for despair.
Yet something different rouses itself inside us....
We remember God.

RUTH SENTER

I have learned to be content in whatever
circumstances I am.... I have learned
the secret of being filled and going hungry,
both of having abundance
and suffering need. I can do all things
through Him who strengthens me.

PHILIPPIANS 4:11–13 NASB

Infinite Love

Fullness of joy is discovered only in the emptying of will....
I can empty because counting His graces has awakened
me to how He cherishes me, holds me, passionately
values me. I can empty because I am full of His love.

ANN VOSKAMP

An infinite God can give all of Himself to each
of His children. He does not distribute Himself
that each may have a part, but to each one He gives
all of Himself as fully as if there were no others....
His love has not changed. It hasn't cooled off,
and it needs no increase because He
has already loved us with infinite love.

A. W. TOZER

Turn around and believe that the good news
that we are loved is better than we ever dared hope,
and that to believe in that good news,
to live out of it and toward it, to be in love
with that good news, is of all glad things
in this world the gladdest thing of all.

FREDERICK BUECHNER

*May you be able to feel and understand...
how long, how wide, how deep,
and how high his love really is.*

EPHESIANS 3:18–19 TLB

A Life of Purpose

Happiness is living by inner purpose,
not by outer pressures.

DAVID AUGSBERGER

Have a purpose in life, and having it, throw into your work
such strength of mind and muscle as God has given you.

THOMAS CARLYLE

The patterns of our days are always rearranging...
and each design for living is unique,
graced with its own special beauty.
The purpose of life is a life of purpose.

ROBERT BYRNE

The meaning of earthly existence lies,
not as we have grown used to thinking,
in prospering, but in the development of the soul.

ALEKSANDR SOLZHENITSYN

Service is the rent we each pay for living.
It is not something to do in your spare time;
it is the very purpose of life.

MARIAN WRIGHT EDELMAN

We know that all things work together for
good to them that love God, to them who
are the called according to his purpose.

ROMANS 8:28 KJV

A Life Transformed

For God is, indeed, a wonderful Father who longs to pour
out His mercy upon us, and whose majesty is so great
that He can transform us from deep within.

TERESA OF AVILA

A philosophy may explain difficult things,
but has no power to change them.
The gospel, the story of Jesus's life, promises change.

PHILIP YANCEY

To pray is to change. This is a great grace.
How good of God to provide a path whereby
our lives can be taken over by love and joy
and peace and patience and kindness and goodness
and faithfulness and gentleness and self-control.

RICHARD J. FOSTER

A life transformed by the power of God
is always a marvel and a miracle.

GERALDINE NICHOLAS

Love is the only force capable
of transforming an enemy into a friend.

MARTIN LUTHER KING JR.

Create in me a clean heart,
O God; and renew a right spirit within me.

PSALM 51:10 KJV

Faith

Faith, as the Bible defines it, is present-tense action.
Faith means being sure of what we hope for...now.
It means knowing something is real, this moment,
all around you, even when you don't see it.
Great faith isn't the ability to believe long and far
into the misty future. It's simply taking God
at His word and taking the next step.

JONI EARECKSON TADA

Optimism is the faith that leads to achievement.
Nothing can be done without hope and confidence.

HELEN KELLER

Whatever happens, do not lose hold
of the two main ropes of life—hope and faith.

Now faith is being sure of what we hope
for and certain of what we do not see....
By faith we understand that the universe
was formed at God's command, so that
what is seen was not made out of what was
visible.... And without faith it is impossible
to please God, because anyone who comes
to him must believe that he exists and that
he rewards those who earnestly seek him.

HEBREWS 11:1, 3, 6 NIV

*Joy is the heart's
harmonious response
to the Lord's song of love.*

A. W. TOZER

Creation Praises

Morning has broken like the first morning.
Blackbird has spoken like the first bird....
Praise with elation, praise every morning,
God's re-creation of the new day!

ELEANOR FARJEON

When morning gilds the skies,
my heart awakening cries:
may Jesus Christ be praised!

JOSEPH BARNBY

Does not all nature around me praise God?
If I were silent, I should be an exception to the universe.
Does not the thunder praise Him as it rolls like drums
in the march of the God of armies? Do not the mountains
praise Him when the woods upon their summits wave
in adoration? Does not the lightning write His name
in letters of fire? Has not the whole earth a voice?
And shall I, can I, silent be?

C. H. SPURGEON

O God, great and wonderful, who has created the heavens,
dwelling in the light and beauty of it...teach me to praise
You, even as the lark which offers her song at daybreak.

ISIDORE OF SEVILLE

Before the mountains were born
or You gave birth to the earth
and the world, even from everlasting
to everlasting, You are God.

PSALM 90:2 NASB

Everyday Prayer

Prayer is such an ordinary, everyday, mundane thing.
Certainly, people who pray are no more saints than
the rest of us. Rather, they are people who want to share
a life with God, to love and be loved, to speak and to listen,
to work and to be at rest in the presence of God.

ROBERTA BONDI

Nothing in your daily life is so insignificant
and so inconsequential that God
will not help you by answering your prayer.

OLE HALLESBY

Can we find a friend so faithful,
who will all our sorrows share?
Jesus knows our every weakness:
take it to the Lord in prayer.

GEORGE SCRIVEN

Prayer should be the key of the day
and the lock of the night.

*Cast your burden on the LORD,
and He shall sustain you: He shall never
permit the righteous to be moved.*

PSALM 55:22 NKJV

Unconditional Love

There is nothing we can do that will make God
love us less, and there's nothing we can do
that will make Him love us more. He will always
and forever love us unconditionally. What He wants
from us is that we love Him back with all our heart.

Do not dwell upon your inner failings.... Just do this:
Bring your soul to the Great Physician—
exactly as you are, even and especially
at your worst moment.... For it is in such moments
that you will most readily sense His healing presence.

TERESA OF AVILA

God will never let you be shaken
or moved from your place near His heart.

JONI EARECKSON TADA

If you have a special need today, focus your full attention
on the goodness and greatness of your Father
rather than on the size of your need.
Your need is so small compared to His ability to meet it.

*My grace is sufficient for you: for My
strength is made perfect in weakness.*

2 CORINTHIANS 12:9 NKJV

God Is Our Refuge

When you accept the fact that sometimes seasons are dry
and times are hard and that God is in control of both,
you will discover a sense of divine refuge, because the hope
then is in God and not in yourself.

CHARLES R. SWINDOLL

Christian hope is a different sort of thing from other kinds.
The Greek word used in the New Testament for hope was
one which in classical literature could mean expectation of
good or bad, but was used by Christians to mean that in
which one confides, or to which one flees for refuge.

ELISABETH ELLIOT

When God has become...our refuge and our fortress, then we can reach out to Him in the midst of a broken world and feel at home while still on the way.

HENRI J. M. NOUWEN

My soul, wait in silence for God only,
For my hope is from Him....
On God my salvation and my glory rest;
the rock of my strength,
my refuge is in God.

PSALM 62:5, 7 NASB

Showers of Blessings

The sun...in its full glory, either at rising or setting—
this, and many other like blessings we enjoy daily;
and for the most of them, because they are so common,
most men forget to pay their praises. But let not us.

IZAAK WALTON

God, who is love—who is, if I may say it this way,
made out of love—simply cannot help
but shed blessing on blessing upon us.

HANNAH WHITALL SMITH

Gratitude can transform common days
into thanksgivings, turn routine jobs into joy,
and change ordinary opportunities into blessings.

WILLIAM ARTHUR WARD

A miracle is when the whole is greater than the sum of its parts. A miracle is when one plus one equals a thousand.

FREDERICK BUECHNER

In difficulties, I can drink freely of God's power
and experience His touch of refreshment and blessing—
much like an invigorating early spring rain.

*In the proper season
I will send the showers they need.
There will be showers of blessing.*

EZEKIEL 34:26 NLT

Special Gifts

Every person ever created is so special that their presence
in the world makes it richer and fuller and more wonderful
than it could ever have been without them.

Where you are right now is God's place for you.
Live and obey and love and believe right there.

1 CORINTHIANS 7:17 MSG

We were not sent into this world to do anything
into which we cannot put our hearts.

JOHN RUSKIN

Use what talents you possess: the woods would be
very silent if no birds sang there except those that sang best.

HENRY VAN DYKE

God gives everyone a special gift
and a special place to use it.

The joy that you give to others
is the joy that comes back to you.

JOHN GREENLEAF WHITTIER

Every good and perfect gift is from above,
coming down from the Father
of the heavenly lights, who does not change
like shifting shadows.

JAMES 1:17 NIV

I look up and try to understand
that our solar system is a tiny
pinprick in that great river
of stars.... The truth I hold to
is that it is all God's, joyfully
created, and that it is good.

MADELEINE L'ENGLE

Completely Loved

I pray that God, the source of hope,
will fill you completely with joy and peace
because you trust in him. Then you will overflow
with confident hope through the power of the Holy Spirit.

ROMANS 15:13 NLT

We are of such value to God
that He came to live among us...
and to guide us home. He will go to any length to seek us....
We can only respond by loving God for His love.

CATHERINE OF SIENA

Every one of us as human beings is known and loved
by the Creator apart from every other human on earth.

JAMES DOBSON

You are valuable just because you exist.
Not because of what you do or what you have done,
but simply because you are. Just think about the way
Jesus honors you...and smile.

MAX LUCADO

We love him, because he first loved us.

1 JOHN 4:19 KJV

God With Us

It is God's knowledge of me, His careful husbanding
of the ground of my being, His constant presence
in the garden of my little life that guarantees my joy.

W. PHILLIP KELLER

God gets down on His knees among us; gets on our level
and shares Himself with us. He does not reside afar off
and send diplomatic messages, He kneels among us....
God shares Himself generously and graciously.

EUGENE PETERSON

Let your faith in Christ, the omnipresent One,
be in the quiet confidence that He will every day
and every moment keep you as the apple of His eye.

ANDREW MURRAY

You are in the Beloved...therefore infinitely dear
to the Father, unspeakably precious to Him.
You are never, not for one second, alone.

NORMAN DOWTY

God bless you and utterly satisfy your heart...with Himself.

AMY CARMICHAEL

We are never more fulfilled than when our longing
for God is met by His presence in our lives.

BILLY GRAHAM

*My Presence will go with you,
and I will give you rest.*

EXODUS 33:14 NIV

Your Unique Message

You have a unique message to deliver,
a unique song to sing, a unique act of love to bestow.
This message, this song, and this act of love
have been entrusted exclusively to the one and only you.

JOHN POWELL

When the dream in our heart is one that God
has planted there, a strange happiness flowers into us.
At that moment all of the spiritual resources of the universe
are released to help us. Our praying is then at one
with the will of God and becomes a channel for the Creator's
always joyous, triumphant purposes for us and our world.

CATHERINE MARSHALL

We have missed the full impact of the gospel
if we have not discovered what it is to be ourselves,
loved by God, irreplaceable in His sight,
unique among our fellowmen.

BRUCE LARSON

Life with God is an individual matter,
and general formulas do not easily apply.

PHILIP YANCEY

Isn't everything you have and everything
you are sheer gifts from God?

1 CORINTHIANS 4:7 MSG

His Presence

When God finds a soul that rests in Him and is not easily
moved...to this same soul He gives the joy of His presence.

CATHERINE OF GENOA

Know by the light of faith that God is present,
and be content with directing all your actions toward Him.

BROTHER LAWRENCE

"Blessed are the pure in heart for they shall see God."
Meaning? They will see God work. They will see Him
in their lives. They will feel His presence.

CHARLES R. SWINDOLL

It is when things go wrong, when good things
do not happen, when our prayers seem to have been lost,
that God is most present.

Madeleine L'Engle

God wants us to be present where we are.
He invites us to see and to hear what is around us and,
through it all, to discern the footprints of the Holy.

Richard J. Foster

If I rise on the wings of the dawn,
if I settle on the far side of the sea,
even there your hand will guide me,
your right hand will hold me fast.

Psalm 139:9–10 NIV

Joy Is

Joy is the touch of God's finger.
The object of our longing is not the touch
but the Toucher. This is true of all good things—
they are all God's touch. Whatever we desire,
we are really desiring God.

PETER KREEFT

For I am bound with fleshly bands,
Joy, beauty, lie beyond my scope;
I strain my heart, I stretch my hands,
And catch at hope.

CHRISTINA ROSSETTI

Joy is really a road sign pointing us to God.
Once we have found God...we no longer need
to trouble ourselves so much about the quest for joy.

C. S. LEWIS

A joyful heart is like a sunshine of God's love,
the hope of eternal happiness, a burning flame of God.

MOTHER TERESA

Joy is the echo of God's life within us.

Be joyful. Grow to maturity. Encourage each other. Live in harmony and peace. Then the God of love and peace will be with you.

2 CORINTHIANS 13:11 NLT

Treasure in Nature

If we are children of God, we have a tremendous treasure
in nature and will realize that it is holy and sacred.
We will see God reaching out to us in every wind that blows,
every sunrise and sunset, every cloud in the sky,
every flower that blooms, and every leaf that fades.

OSWALD CHAMBERS

The longer I live, the more my mind dwells
upon the beauty and the wonder of the world.

JOHN BURROUGHS

Look up at all the stars in the night sky and hear
your Father saying, "I carefully set each one in its place.
Know that I love you more than these." Sit by the lake's
edge, listening to the water lapping the shore and hear
your Father gently calling you to that place near His heart.

The heavens are telling the glory of God;
they are a marvelous display
of his craftsmanship.

PSALM 19:1 TLB

Each day is a treasure box
of gifts from God,
just waiting to be opened.
Open your gifts with excitement.
You will find forgiveness
attached to ribbons of joy.
You will find love wrapped
in sparkling gems.

JOAN CLAYTON